BUTTON SOUP

A Cookbook for Young Cut and Paste Chefs

Welcome to Button Soup,

This cookbook has been a dream of mine for a very long time. It is a collection of recipes that will never be eaten but will always be fun to make and play with! Each recipe is a project for young ones who love arts and crafts as well as pretending with playmates, dolls and their stuffed toys. As a safety precaution, nothing in any recipe includes something edible — so the youngsters should not be confused that these are only pretend and play activities.

Note that many recipes need the help of an older person for steps such as finding the materials needed, cutting with scissors, gluing, slicing clay with a knife, etc. so scan through them and make note. There are blank recipe cards at the end of each chapter for you and the little ones to create your very own recipes - be sure to use them!

Also, note that there are suggested fun songs to sing as the little chef works—you will find a starter list of songs at the end of the book. Search on YouTube for any songs you are unfamiliar with.

Have fun!
Jane

I would love to hear from you about how the recipes turn out—or even see pictures that you upload to my blog on
www.tinkeringwithjoy.com or email tinkeringwithjoy@yahoo.com

BUTTON SOUP
A cookbook for the little cut and paste chefs who shop at the craft store

Jane McGreevy Schenck

TABLE OF CONTENTS

SOUPS
Alphabet Soup 6
Frothy, Froggie Giggle Goop Soup 8
Button Soup and Saltines 10
Curlique Lady-Bug Stew 12
Yum Yum Gumbo 14

SALADS
Berry Berry Good Salad 20
Cookie Salad 22
Kookie, Cukey Silly Salad 24
Classy, Grassy Yard Goodies Salad 26

ENTREES
Spaghetti and Pretty Balls 32
Noodle Kaboodle Crunch-a-Bunch 34
Musical Macaroni 36
Sea Shell Pizza 38
Squishy, Swooshie Sushi 40

DESSERTS
Pink Pom Pom Pearl Parfait 46
Jiggly Jubilation Jello 48
Cutie Pie Pie 50
Sun Toasted, Honey Roasted Rosey Poseys 52
Sweet Pea Baby Cakes 54
Princess Jewel Cakelettes 56

RESOURCES
Ingredients to stock up on 62
Pots, Pans, Bowls, Dishes 64
Templates 66
Sources 67
Songs to Cook By 68

This book is dedicated to:
Aunt Jenny and Aunt Betty who opened up their door to sunshine and whimsey.
and
Raegan, Claire, Henry, Emma & Luke who are growing now in their sunshine years!

Published by Homing Instinct, LLC.
Pittsburgh, PA

First Edition
ISBN: 978-0-692-17470-8

© 2018. All rights reserved.
No part of this book may be used or reproduced in any manner whatsoever without written permission except in the case of brief quotation embodied in critical articles or reviews. Contact the author at tinkeringwithjoy@yahoo.com.

SOUPS

Ingredients

- Alphabet letters (small; mixed styles - 3-4 different kinds)
- Floral "pebbles"
- Soup pot, spoon & ladle
- Serving bowls

Directions...

1. Add the different kinds or letters to the soup pot. Stir, counting to 15.

2. Pour a little bit of floral pebbles into the pot. Don't worry that they fall to the bottom.

3. Put the pot under a lamp to simmer in its light.

4. When it smells done, gather your guests and serve!

Alphabet Soup

Frothy, Froggie Giggle Goop Soup

Ingredients

- Big handful of white crinkle paper
- As many little froggies as you can round up
- White play foam
- Butter knife
- Shaker of glitter
- Serving bowls

Directions...

1. Put a little bit of white crinkle paper in each bowl.
2. Add a few frogs in each bowl
3. Here is the fun part: with your fingers or the butter knife, begin putting white foam around the rim of each bowl.
4. Even out the rim of foam.
5. Call your guests to eat and be prepared for frog antics.
6. Offer the glitter shaker in case someone wants seasoning.

Ingredients

- Jar of buttons (gathered from Moms and Aunts and everyone)
- Big handful of tiny pompoms
- Glitter (any color) shaker
- Soup tureen and ladle
- Bowls for guests
- One 10" x 12" piece of ivory felt and ivory thread and needle (for saltines to be prepared ahead of time)

NOTE: The felt saltines need to be made before this recipe is made.

Directions...

Plan for the saltines to be made ahead of time. Using the template on page 64, cut six squares from the felt, to make 3 saltines. Placing two squares together for the first cracker, use blanket stitch around all four sides. Finish with the rows of tiny knots. Repeat for the other two crackers.

1. Now that you have saltines, you can begin to make the soup!

2. Pour out the buttons and pick out the 30 or so prettiest, yummiest ones.

3. Add them to the soup tureen.

4. Scoop out about 15 tiny pompoms and add to the soup.

5. Stir well.

6. Sniff a spoonful to see how much longer the soup needs to simmer. Waiting is more fun with a funny song to sing.

7. Once the soup is ready, call your guests and serve!

Curlique Ladybug Stew

Ingredients

- About 4 to 6 thick and colorful pipe cleaners, each cut into 3 almost equal lengths
- Pencil
- Pretend Lady-Bugs
- Big soup bowl
- Serving spoon
- Bowls for guests

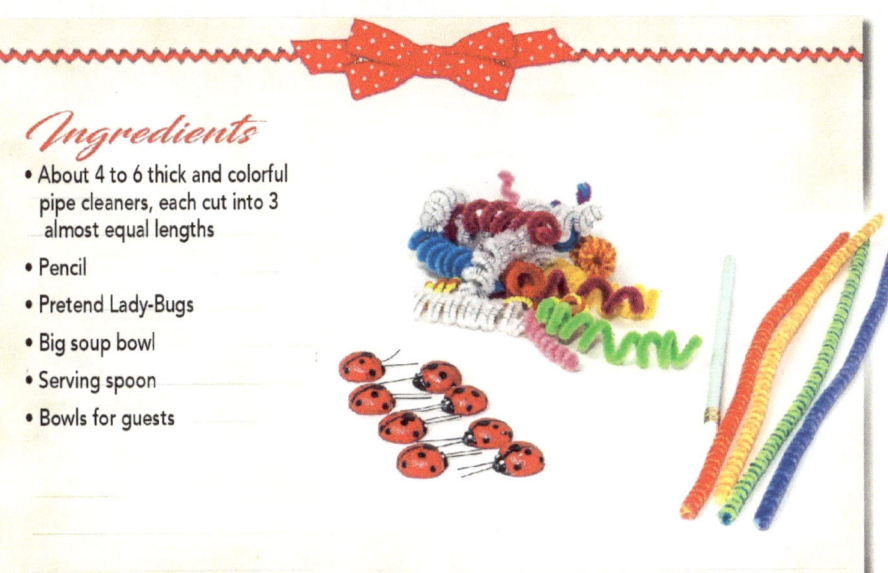

Directions...

1. Wind each piece of pipe cleaner tightly around the pencil. Then slide the curlique off.

2. Add curliques into the soup bowls.

3. You might like to hold a springy curlique between your thumb and fore finger to test its spring-i-ness. If any need tightened, put it back onto the pencil and wind it tighter.

4. Carefully add the Lady-bugs into the stew and whisper a song about Lady-bugs to them so they will stay and play.

5. Scoop the stew into your guests' bowls.

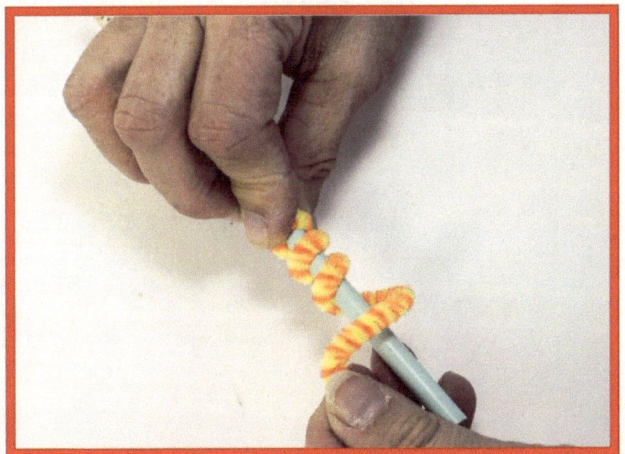

Ingredients

- Two-three handfuls of interesting little things from a yard or park,
  - --stored in a jar or small bag
- Try to find small plastic (but friendly) bugs
- Real or artificial ferns or leaves
- Just a small bit of Sand (any color)
- Small crock pot and lid
- Serving spoon

Directions ...

1. Examine the natural and wholesome goodies gathered from outside. Decide which you will use in today's gumbo.

2. Carefully lay them in the crock pot so nothing breaks

3. Add plastic bugs, if you have any

4. Tuck in pieces of ferns or leaves

5. Add just a little sand and close up the container of sand.

6. No need to stir this lovely combo of gumbo

7. Just spoon the stew into each bowl and serve

Yum-Yum Gumbo

Here's My Recipe

Directions...

Here's My Recipe

Directions ...

Here's My Recipe

Directions...

Berry, Berry Good Salad

Ingredients

* Artificial Berries: raspberries, strawberries, any berries
- Artificial leaves, ferns
- Large serving container
- Serving tongs (or two spoons)
- Guests' plates or bowls

Directions...

1. Assemble all of your berries and leaves, like grown-up chefs do when they begin to work, in neat piles

2. Arrange berries and leaves in the large serving dish.

3. Using salad tongs, place salad in each person's bowl. Carefully and gently, arrange the berries one at a time. Add in a leaf or 2 or 3 every so often. Make sure each bowl looks pretty enough to gobble up.

4. Decide what song you will lead your guests in singing at this lovely berry party.

5. Call your guests to eat.

Ingredients

- Air drying clay (any brand) & plastic sandwich bag
- Tiny cookie cutters
- Glitter pens of pretty colors (or clear glue and loose glitter)
- Cookie platter
  (Cookies need to be prepared a day ahead of time, so the glitter decoration can dry)
- Artificial cookies
  (Christmas tree ornaments)
- Silk flower lettuce leaves
- Bowls for each guest

Directions...

1. Plan to make the cookies a full day ahead of time. You will use the air-drying clay, the cookie cutters, a platter to put the cookies on and the glitter pens.

2. Take a handful of clay but then seal the rest in a plastic sandwich bag to keep it from hardening.

3. Work the clay to soften it. Roll it into a ball and then flatten the ball. You can flatten it into a circle to be very thin with the palm of your hand. Stretch and flatten the circle. Turn the piece of clay over and it will be very smooth!

4. Using the cookie cutters, cut out as many cookies as you can and set them onto the platter making sure that they do not touch each other.

5. Left-over clay can be rolled up into another ball and flattened to let you make a few more cookies. If there is any left-over clay you can save it in the sealed bag.

6. Now you can decorate each cookie with the squeezable glitter pens.

7. Let them dry overnight. (If you are using clear glue instead, make thin lines in the shape you want and carefully tap small stream of glitter onto the glue. Do not remove extra glitter until tomorrow when the decorations have dried. Then you can tap the extra glitter into a bowl—and possibly put it back into its container.)

8. The next day you can create the salad --- put lettuce leaves in each guest's dish and tuck a few cookies inside. Serve!

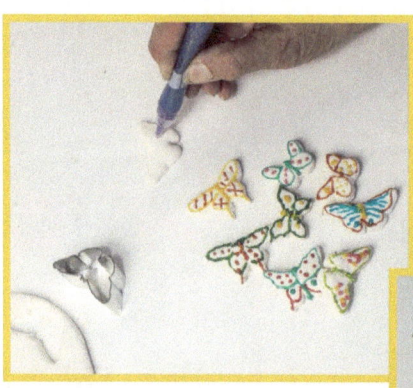

Cookie Salad

Kookie Cukey Silly Salad

Ingredients

- Air drying clay & plastic sandwich bag
- Serated edge knife for an adult to use
- Dark green felt tip marker
- Two thick pipe cleaners
- Pencil
- Two sets of googly eyes and glue
- Small feathers
- Balloon pieces (or rubber bands) cut into small pieces
- Confetti sprinkles
- Large salad bowl
- Cupcake papers for serving dishes

Directions ...

1. Plan to make the cucumber slices the day before so the air- drying clay will have time to dry out. Take a handful of clay, then seal the rest in a plastic sandwich bag to keep it from hardening.

2. Work the clay to soften it. Roll it into a ball and then shape it into a long cucumber about 2-1/2" thick.

3. An older person needs to use a knife to slice 5-6 pieces of the cucumber. The knife may "crush" the cucumber slice but, shape the clay back into its circular form.

4. Refer to the cucumber design in the templates on page 64 to draw the "insides".

5. Color the edge of each slice dark green. Repeat the drawing of the cucumber seeds on the end of the unsliced clay and shade the whole outer skin with the felt tip marker.

6. Let all of the cucumber parts dry over-night.

7. Next day: you can begin preparing this dish by making the wooly bugs: wrapping pipe cleaners around the pencil and gluing on googly eyes.

8. Put pretend lettuce into the bowls or cupcake papers and keep all extra in the larger salad bowl.

9. Add balloon pieces or rubber bands to the guests' bowls and remaining amount to the bigger salad dish.

10. Place 2-3 cucumber slices into each guests' bowl.

11. Sprinkle confetti 'salt' to taste!

Ingredients

- Dried, feathery flower stalks (6-8 stalks altogether)
- Clover blossoms (real or artificial)
- Silk flower leafy greens
- 4 pretty feathers
- Taller bowls for serving guests (candle holders will work)

Directions ...

1. Place greens in the bowls, to line the inner edges
2. Gently pull the stalks from the plant.
3. Put 4 or 5 stalks in each guest's bowl. (They will help keep the greenery in place)
4. Drop a few clover blossom heads into each bowl
5. Add two pretty feathers and invite guests to use them as chop sticks!
6. Serve

Classy Grassy Yard Goodies Salad

Here's My Recipe

Directions ...

Here's My Recipe

Directions...

Here's My Recipe

Ingredients

Directions ...

ENTREES

Spaghetti & Pretty Balls

Ingredients

- Iridescent white curling ribbon, cut into thirty 18" strips
- Scissors (for an adult to curl the ribbon strips)
- Air drying clay & plastic bag
- Decorative ribbon or pretend jewels
- Clear glue
- Pot for spaghetti
- Tiny colander
- Pan and Utensils
- Serving plates

Directions...

1. Before you begin this recipe, an adult needs to cut the ribbon strips and 'curl' them with a scissors blade. You can keep the spaghetti in the colander.

2. Open the air drying clay and break off a handful. Put the rest of it in the plastic bag to stay moist.

3. Break up the clay into equal sizes to be rolled into balls about 1.5" thick.

4. How will you decorate your "pretty balls"? Use the pictures here to inspire you. Some stickers or pretend jewels come with a sticky back side, but they must be glued on with very small amounts of glue.

5. While decorating them, you can pretend to "fry" them in the pan, rolling around, "browning them".

6. To prepare your guests' plates, first place a small pile of ribbon spaghetti on each and then top with 2-3 pretty balls.

7. Enjoy!!

NOTE: An adult needs to prepare curling robon ahead of time. Make about thirty (30) 18" strips. Cut and curl with a scissor blade.

Ingredients

- Pink crinkle paper
- Pink floral stones
- Mixed colored plastic jewels
- Stars of heavy cardboard —about twenty 2" high
- Glitter in a shaker
- Small casserole dish
- Plates for guests

Directions...

1. Put crinkle paper in the casserole dish
2. Stand the stars up all around the dish
3. Spread the stones and jewels throughout the casserole
4. Sprinkle a small bit of glitter on top of the contents
5. Let it cook under a lamp for as long as it takes to sing one or two pink happy songs!
6. Smell to see if it is cooked well enough
7. Serve on the plates and call your guests to the table!

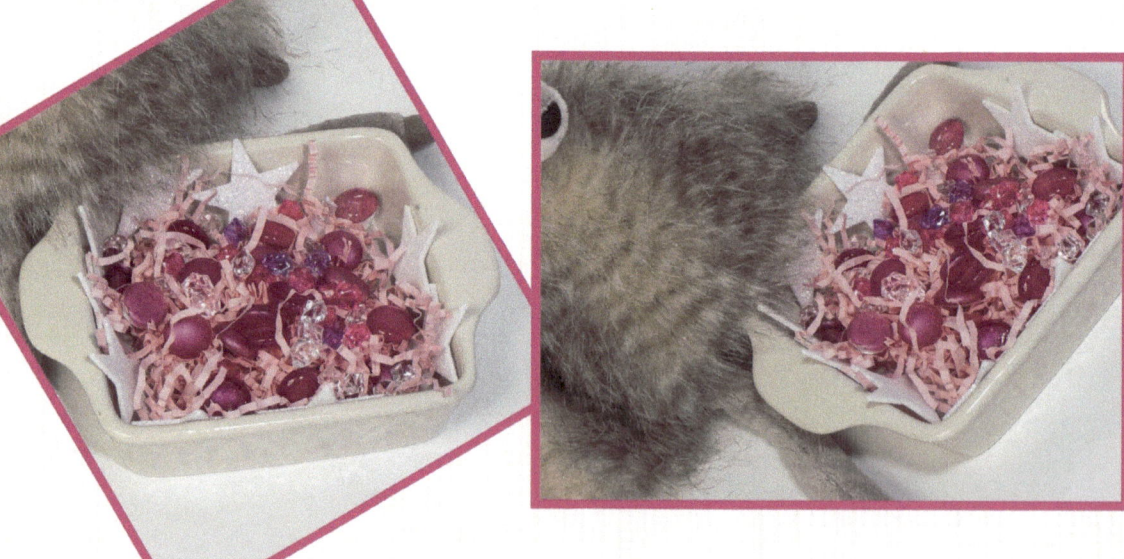

Noodle Kaboodle Crunch A Bunch Casserole

Musical Macaroni

Ingredients

- Four pretty and thick pipe cleaners (cut into 2" lengths)
- Small handful of tiny jingle bells
- Musical Notes (cut out or find scrap-booking stickers)
- Measuring spoons
- Covered casserole pot
- Serving bowls

Directions...

1. Have an adult cut all of the pipe cleaners into 2" strips

2. Bend each of the short pipe cleaners into a C shape and place into the casserole (singing makes the time fly by)

3. Add two T. (tablespoons) of small jingle bells to the casserole

4. Add musical notes (about 15)

5. Stir well.

6. Cover and place on a window sill where the sun will slowly bake the casserole.

7. Sing a silly songs while you wait.

8. Smell to see if the casserole has finished cooking.

9. When it smells just right, serve !

Ingredients

- Air drying clay & plastic bag
- Butter knife
- Acrylic paint: one that looks like the color of pizza dough, and one sky blue
- Paint brushes (to be cleaned under running water)
- Small jar of Gel Medium (to add thickness and shine)
- Small jar (with lid) for mixing
- Measuring spoons
- Bag of tiny sea shells
- Serving dishes

Directions...

1. Pull enough air drying clay off to make a round ball 3" wide. Put the remainder into the plastic bag.

2. Knead the clay and roll into a ball.

3. Flatten it with your palm into a circle and continue stretching it out until it measures about 5" wide. Turn it over and find the smooth surface.

4. Using the butter knife, make a cross design gently into the dough (being careful not to break the pieces apart). This makes 4 big pieces. Next, put an X in the middle of the cross. This should look like the way real pizza is scored. You might want to finger press a crust around the outside of the dough.

5. Then paint top of the crust with paint color the color of dough. Using the butter knife again, cut and remove 2 or 3 pieces. Let all of the pieces dry over night.

6. When you are ready, open the Gel Medium and spoon two T. (tablespoons) of it into jar. Then put only one T. (tablespoon) of sea blue paint into the jar. Mix thoroughly with the end of a paintbrush. It should look thick like icing—the ocean sauce for a sea shell pizza!.

7. Apply this fluffy paint on top of the dough as if you were icing a cake and leaving little peaks.

8. Place sea shells into the paint where they will dry in place.

9. Wait over-night for this wonderful dish!

Sea Shell Pizza

PLEASE NOTE:
This recipe takes two days and two nights to make.

Squishy, Swooshie Sushi

Ingredients

- Pretty colors of "floam"
- Fancy colors of paper
- Scissors (for adult to use)
- Clear glue
- Tiny snips of felt pieces
- Artificial blades of grass
- Straight pins
- Platter for the sushi
- Serving dishes

Directions...

1. Find a book or website that shows pictures of sushi, and study them to see what designs you would like to make.

2. Cut strips of your fancy paper approximately 1" high and 4" long. Templates for wraps of the sushi pieces on page 64.

3. First form the outer wall of each piece. You may need to overlap ends and glue the wrap closed. Pushing a few straight pins in, where it's glued, will help keep it closed while the glue dries.

4. Make sure the glue on the wraps is dried. Carefully add bits of play foam inside. Fill up the space but be careful not break the wall apart.

5. Ask an adult to cut tiny pieces of colored felt. Get ideas for decorative toppings from below. Put the itsy bitsy colorful pieces of felt.... into the center of each piece. Glue them down.

6. No waiting-- set out the delectable fresh sushi for your guests!

41

Here's My Recipe

Directions...

Here's My Recipe

Directions…

Here's My Recipe

Directions...

DESSERTS

Ingredients

- Pearls galore—white, pink, any and all sizes
- Pink pompoms—different shades
- Large bowl
- Spoon
- Parfait glasses or pretty bowls

Directions...

1. Put the pompoms into the bowl.

2. Then pour pearls into the bowl, slowly, since if they spill, they are difficult to round up!

3. Stir the ingredients but do not be surprised if the pearls stay at the bottom. They do because they are heavier than the pompoms. But stir them for the fun of it!

4. This is a one song stirring job. Pick a fun one!

5. Once you are finished, spoon the yummy mix carefully into the parfait glasses.

6. Call your guests to feast their eyes and imagine how strawberry-ish this dessert smells!

Pink Pom Pom Pearl Parfait

Jiggly Jubilation Jello

Ingredients

- A package of pink "water jewels" (also called water pearls)
- Container or bowl to hold water
- Teaspoons
- Optional: A pretend grasshopper
- Artificial lettuce leaves
- Serving spoon
- Bowls for guests

Directions...

1. Open the package of water jewels and pour an amount as small as three pennies. Close the bag.

2. Add 3 T. (tablespoons) of water to the beads. No need to stir. But you do need to be patient because it will take a few hours for the tiny beads to absorb water and enlarge.

3. It will be easy to tell when this task is done—the beads will be much bigger and shiny because they are full of water!

4. Place an artificial lettuce leaf (or two if they are small) in each guest's bowl. But do not spoon the "Ju-Ju Jello beads" yet....

5. So, if you are curious about why to invite a grasshopper to this event, now is the time you will find out: grasshoppers love to dance on squishy things. But, you will need to sing for her to dance, so pick a happy song! Place yours into the bowl holding the beads, and encourage her to do the jiggly dance among the beads.

6. Now, you may spoon the beads onto the lettuce leaves and let the mmmmm-mmm good humming begin.

Note: The water jewels can be saved in a jar. If they begin to shrink, just add a small amount of water

Ingredients

- 2-4 Small tart/ pie pans
- Air drying clay & plastic sandwich bag
- Many, many small silk flowers
- Many tiny bows and hearts

Directions...

1. Open the air drying clay and pull off a small section to roll into a ball. Keep the rest in the package and put the package into a plastic bag so it stays moist.

2. Roll it into a ball and then press it down into a circle with your palm. Stretch it out to be the shape of pie crust.

3. Carefully roll up a small part, pick it up in one piece and place the crust into the pie pan.

4. Gently press it down and make little smushes for the crust edge.

5. Repeat these steps to make a 2nd pie dough.

6. Let the pie dough dry overnight.

7. You can paint the crust or leave it white.

8. Now, you can put the little flowers inside, arranged any way you like. For fun, make up flavors for the different colors of blossoms!

9. Next, tuck in small bows among the flowers.

10. They need to "bake" in a warm place. Can you find one?

11. When they are finished baking, call you guests!

Cutie Pie Pie

Sun Toasted, Honey Roasted Rosey-Poseys

Ingredients

- Artificial roses that are similar colors but different sizes
- Rack or dish
- "Pretend Honey"
- Glitter (the color of the roses)
- Pretty platter
- Serving dishes

Directions...

1. Remove the roses from the stems, being careful to not get stuck by the thorns.

2. Take leaves off the stem too, keeping them in their set of threes

3. Set the roses on a rack or dish.

4. **Pretend** to drip honey on the roses.

5. Sprinkle glitter sparingly over the roses.

6. Now, it is time to set the roses in the sun to be toasted. If it is sunny, set them where they can absorb the sunlight for one long song's worth of time. If it is not sunny, try to find a lamp to set the roses under in the light, for toasting.

7. Do the sniff test to see if the beautiful dessert is ready to serve.

8. Place a sprig of leaves on a guest's plate to lay along side two pretty roses.

9. Serve!

Ingredients

- Six small brown paper mache boxes
- A few stems of silk flower sweet peas
- A few large soft artificial leaves
- Air drying clay & plastic bag
- Little rolling pin
- White pearl squeeze paint
- Clear glue
- Pinch of green moss
- Serving platter
- Dishes for each guest

Directions ...

1. Pull sweet pea blooms off the stems and set aside.

2. Open the air drying clay and pull off a handful; put the remainder of the clay into a plastic bag so it will not dry out.

3. Divide the clump of clay into 6 even pieces. Soften one at a time into a small thin square shape. Wrap the shape around a small paper mache box and completely smooth the clay on all sides, except the bottom.

4. Repeat this process with the other five small boxes.

5. Let them dry out over-night.

6. Paint the bottoms of the boxes and let dry. Then paint all sides covered in the clay. Let dry thoroughly.

7. Put a small bit of glue on top of one of the boxes then sprinkle moss bits to make a tiny bed for a sweet pea blossom. But the moss needs another small bit of glue on top. Set a sweet pea on the center.

8. *(Optional)* Put tiny baby buttons on the sweet peas. We call these "baby cakes". Bakeries call them petit fours!

9. The baby cakes are ready to enjoy.

Sweet Pea Baby Cakes

55

Princess Jewel Cakelettes

Ingredients

- Ten large cotton balls
- Clear glue
- Princess dress-up jewelry—two necklaces and two bracelets that are strung together with elastic string
- Two "dishes" fit for princess cakes
- Teapot, cups and saucers

Directions...

1. You will be making a small cake "tower" of cotton balls.

2. Doing one cake at a time, lay 4 cotton balls on a plate, close together. Sparingly dot glue along the sides of the cotton balls so they form the first layer of the cakelette. Let dry.

3. Next, lay 3 cotton balls on top of them and glue.

4. Finally lay 2 balls on top of the three and secure with glue. Make sure all glue is dried before continuing.

5. Pick up one necklace, turn it into an 8 shape, fold in half, with the top and bottom on top of each other.

6. Place this two layer necklace down onto the first and second layer of cotton ball cake.

7. Next turn the bracelet into an 8 shape also and ease it on down to hold the top and middle layer of cotton ball cake together. Doesn't this look pretty?

8. Repeat these steps for the second cake-lette

9. If you and your guest have princess dress-up outfits, it is time to put them on!!

10. Invite your guest to the party table, pour the pretend tea and enjoy the wonderful "vanilla" jewel cakelettes!

Here's My Recipe

Directions...

Here's My Recipe

Ingredients

Directions...

Here's My Recipe

Ingredients

Directions...

Resources

Ingredients to Stock-Up

Pots, Pans, Bowls, Dishes

Templates

Songs to Cook By

SOURCES
A.C. Moore Arts & Crafts www.acmoore.com
Create for Less www.createforless.com
Factory Direct Craft www.factorydirectcraft.com
Michael's Craft Stores www.michaels.com

Ingredients to Stock Up

Small plastic jars are great for holding your favorite ingredients, such as pearls, white glitter, stars, pretty marbles, green sand.....

Another idea - Find cute jars!
Bear jars are sold for baby shower - fill with bath beads, crinkle paper, etc.

Larger jars will be great to hold bigger quantities like feathers, artificial snow, pipe cleaners, leaves, flower buds, bows etc.

These medium sized jars are great for "ingredients" such as more pearls, tiny bells, artificial 4 leaf clovers.

Pots, Pans and Dishes

Have on hand small pots and pans, utensils, tiny dishes - - find them at toy stores, yard sales, etc.

Special, small goodies are found at garage sales, Goodwill stores, grandma's cupboards...

Try Etsy too!

Every hostess would love to have a full set of plates, bowls, cups, glasses, pretend silverware - - these are stocked by IKEA.

Templates

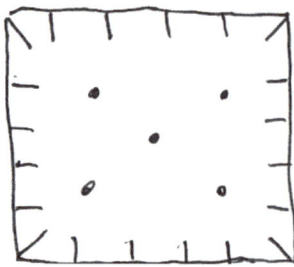

Saltines (pg. 7-8)

1. For each saltine, cut two ivory felt squares and sparse stuffing for the middle.

2. Using ivory thread close the saltine with a blanket stitch.

3. Make french knots where the dots are placed.

Cucumbers (pg. 21-22)

Sushi Wrap (pg. 38-39)

Songs To Cook By

Here is a collection of songs that are fun to sing covering a wide variety of music. Some may be unfamiliar to you, but search to find the words so you and your young chef can both enjoy learning new tunes. You can find each of these songs on YouTube where there are often different versions of the song available to hear! Be sure to add your own favorites to this list!

- The Cuppy Cake Song
- You are my Sunshine
- Hush Little Baby
- Five Little Monkeys Swinging in a Tree
- Baby Bumble Bee
- Kookaburra Sits
- Child of Mine, *Carole King*
- The Muffin Man
- Oh My Darlin' Clementine
- On Top of Spaghetti (aka On Top of Old Smokey)
- Frere Jacques
- Here We Go Looby Lou
- If You're Happy and You Know It
- Home, Home on the Range
- There Was A Crooked Man
- Do Your Ears Hang Low
- Waltzing Matilda
- Take Me Out to the Ballgame
- Oh Dear, What Can the Matter Be?
- Polly, Put the Kettle On
- Oh Where, Oh Where Has My Little Dog Gone
- Heads, Shoulders, Knees and Toes
- Oh Shenandoah
- Polly Wolly Doodle All the Way
- The Lion Sleeps Tonite
- Happy, *Pharrell Williams*
- Story of my Life, *One Direction*
- Sky Full of Stars, *Cold Play*
- Somewhere Over the Rainbow, *Judy Garland*
- What a Wonderful Word, *Louis Armstrong*
- You Raise Me Up, *Josh Groban*
- We Are the World, *USA for Africa 1985*

www.ingramcontent.com/pod-product-compliance
Lightning Source LLC
LaVergne TN
LVHW071032070426
835507LV00003B/124

9780692174708